To Szymon and Inès

Translated from the French *Mille et un oiseaux*

First published in the United Kingdom in 2023 by
Thames & Hudson Ltd, 181A High Holborn, London WC1V 7QX

First published in the United States of America in 2023 by
Thames & Hudson Inc., 500 Fifth Avenue, New York, New York 10110

Original edition © 2022 Actes Sud, Arles
This edition © 2023 Thames & Hudson Ltd, London

British Library Cataloguing-in-Publication Data.
A catalogue record for this book is available from the British Library

Library of Congress Control Number 2022945662

ISBN 978-0-500-65324-1

Printed in China

FSC
www.fsc.org
MIX
Paper from
responsible sources
FSC® C124385

Be the first to know about our new releases,
exclusive content and author events by visiting
thamesandhudson.com
thamesandhudsonusa.com
thamesandhudson.com.au

Joanna Rzezak

1001 BIRDS

A flock of swallows is swooping over a wetland region, full of ponds and reeds. It's a great place for birds to find food.

A **mosquito** makes a delicious snack for a swallow! Swallows love to visit wetlands where they can find lots of their favorite insects to eat, including mosquitoes, crane flies, and dragonflies.

Watch out, duckling! Don't get in the way of the **common crane**. It's fishing in the water for little snails to eat. It also eats seeds, berries, and small insects.

LOOK! There's a **swallow with a red head** on every double page. Try to find her!

The **great crested grebe** is easy to recognize because of the magnificent feathers on its head. It's an excellent diver that can stay under water for up to three minutes.

The great crested grebe builds a floating nest on the water, every year between April and June.

The **mallard** is a very common duck species. It spends a lot of time on the water, using its webbed feet to paddle along.

The part of a tree with branches and leaves is called its crown. It makes an excellent home for lots of different kinds of birds.

When a **starling** wants to make a nest, it finds a hole in a tree. It loves to eat cherries and other fruit, so it's not popular with gardeners!

The starling often steals a hole from another bird to make its nest. It fills the nest with a layer of soft leaves and grass before it lays its eggs. The eggs are pale blue. The starling chicks spend a long time in the nest before they are old enough to live on their own.

The **blackbird** loves to sing. It makes a cone-shaped nest high up in a tree or deep in a hedge.

The **blue tit** can make its nest inside very small holes. This is useful because it means that bigger birds won't try to steal its home! The female blue tit lays around ten eggs at a time. It takes about twenty days for her chicks to grow up and fly away.

The **carrion crow** eats insects, seeds, food scraps and even dead animals.

This **tawny owl** is hiding inside a tree. It is a bird of prey, which means that it hunts and eats smaller creatures. It sleeps during the day and hunts for food at night. It flies silently so its prey can't hear it coming.

This mother swallow is flying home to her nest. Her hungry chicks are waiting for their dinner! She can hear them chirping from a long way away.

The **barn swallow** lives in the countryside. It often makes its nest in a farm, barn, or stable.

There are several different species of swallows. The barn swallow is one of the most common. Its red throat and forked tail make it easy to recognize.

The young swallows learn to fly after twenty days, but they continue to come back to their nest at night for a few months. Flapping their wings is an instinct so they don't need to learn how to do it. However, they must practice landing and steering in the right direction.

A swallow's nest is made from mud, grass, roots, and straw. The inside of the nest is lined with dry grass, feathers, or horsehair. The nest is cup-shaped and is usually built under the roof of a building, joined to a beam or rafter.

The male and female swallows build the nest together. It takes them about a week to finish it. They fly back and forth many times, carrying the building materials they need.

Swallows like to live close to humans. They have made their homes in our buildings and bridges for many thousands of years.

In spring and summer, birds lay their eggs and care for their chicks until they are old enough to look after themselves. When summer ends, some birds want to spend the winter somewhere warmer. This kind of journey is called **migration**. Birds that often migrate include swallows, blackbirds, and starlings.

As the time to migrate grows closer, birds begin to grow restless. They gather in groups in trees and on power lines. They also get ready for their journey by eating more food than usual. This "fuel" will give them energy for their long flight.

The **white stork** builds its big nest in a high place such as a rooftop, a chimney, or an electricity pole. A stork's nest can weigh up to 110 lbs.

Why do birds migrate? For birds, winter means shorter days and less food. When birds feel the weather growing colder, they know that winter is on its way. It's time to fly to a place where it's warmer and where food is easier to find.

Blackbirds

Blue tits

In recent years, scientists have noticed that some birds have stopped migrating. This is caused by **climate change**, which means that winter in some places is not as cold as it used to be.

Some birds migrate just a short distance. Others, such as **barn swallows**, travel all the way from Northern Europe to South Africa, or from North America to South America, a journey of almost 6,000 miles! American barn swallows start their migration in June or July. Some European swallows start their migration in August, but most of them don't set off until September.

As summer ends, the days grow shorter. Migrating birds know it is time to set off on their long journey.

Bar-headed geese form a V-shape when they fly. This helps them save energy. The wind hits the bird at the front of the V, but the birds behind it are protected and don't have to work as hard. The birds take turns being at the front, which means they all get a chance to rest. Canada geese and many ducks and swans also fly in this way.

Flying birds use currents of warm air called **thermals** to push them forward or help them rise.

The bird that holds the record for the longest non-stop flight is the **bar-tailed godwit**. It can fly for more than 7,000 miles without resting.

Migrating birds often fly for thousands of miles. How do they know where to go? Some of them use the sun to guide them, while others watch out for landmarks such as mountains and rivers. There are also some birds that have a special sense called **magnetoreception**. This means that they can feel the Earth's magnetic field and can use it to find their way. Birds with this skill include homing pigeons and European robins.

Who's the highest flyer?

The record for the highest flying bird is held by **Rüppell's vulture**. It can reach a height of around 36,000 feet, which is higher than most planes. It also makes its nest in high places, usually on rocky cliffs. It lives in Africa, but it can sometimes be seen flying through the skies of southern Spain.

A passenger jet flies at a height between 29,500 and 39,500 feet.

The **common crane** can reach a height of 33,000 feet. It usually flies with its long neck and legs stretched out. It has a very loud call that can be heard several miles away. An ancient Greek legend says that the crane sometimes carries a pebble in its mouth to stop itself from making noise and being attacked by eagles.

The **mallard** is a very common species of duck. Male mallards have a green head and a white ring around their neck, making them easy to recognize. The female mallard is brown and slightly smaller than the male. They are very noisy and quack a lot!

The **bar-headed goose** can fly at a height of 33,000 feet. It migrates in groups of between 50 and 200 geese.

There are two main ways for birds to fly: gliding or flapping. The **house sparrow** uses flapping to fly.

Pigeons that have been trained to deliver messages are called **carrier pigeons**. They were used during World War I and World War II as a way of sending secret information. The messages were carried in a small tube, fastened to the pigeon's leg.

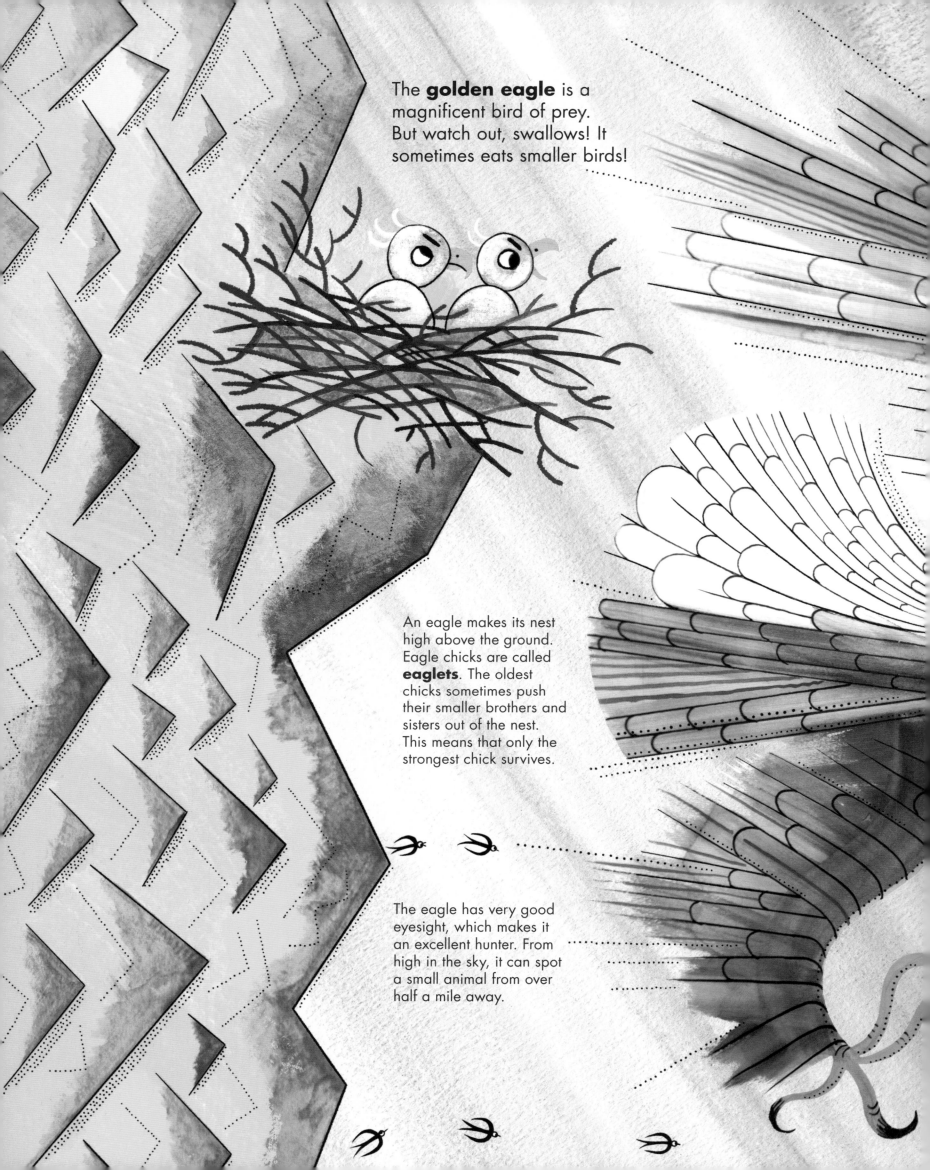

The **golden eagle** is a magnificent bird of prey. But watch out, swallows! It sometimes eats smaller birds!

An eagle makes its nest high above the ground. Eagle chicks are called **eaglets**. The oldest chicks sometimes push their smaller brothers and sisters out of the nest. This means that only the strongest chick survives.

The eagle has very good eyesight, which makes it an excellent hunter. From high in the sky, it can spot a small animal from over half a mile away.

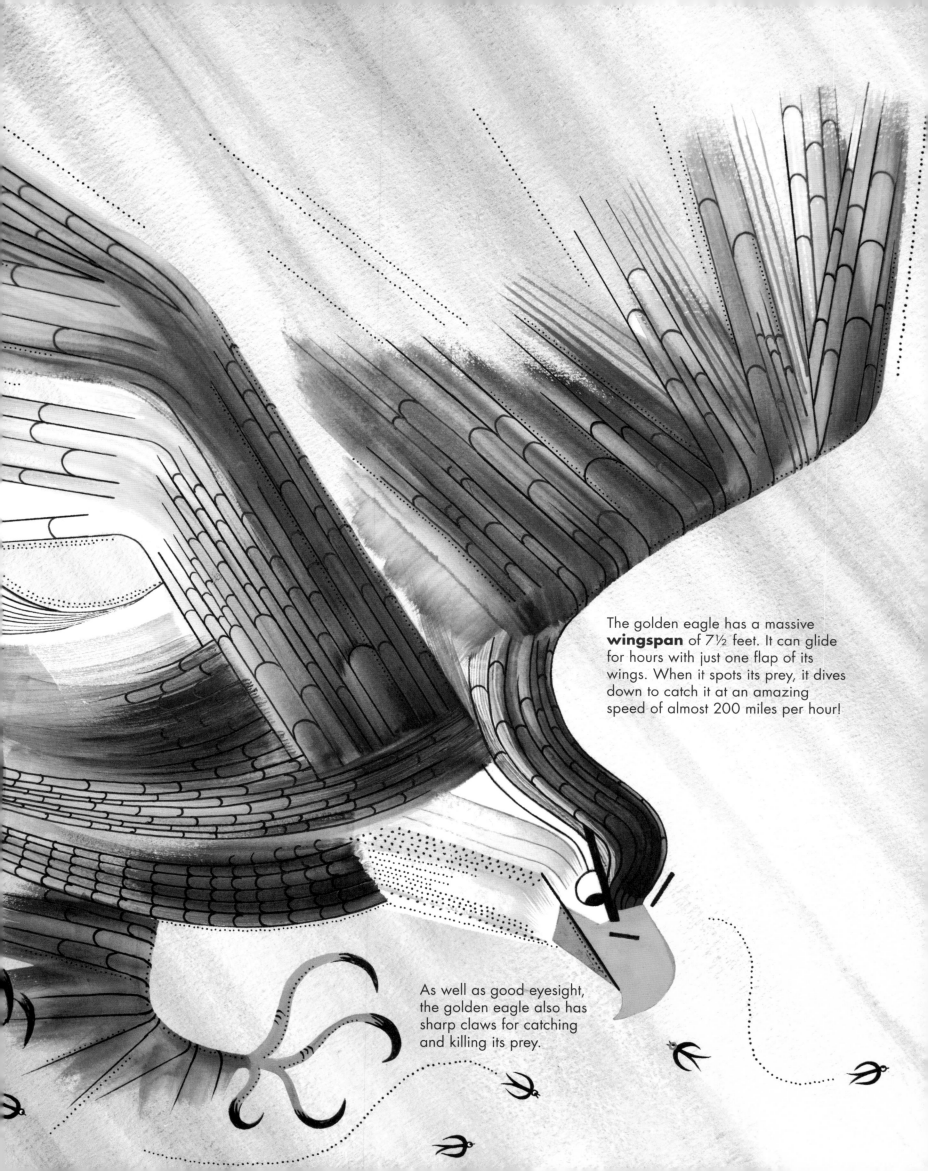

The golden eagle has a massive **wingspan** of 7½ feet. It can glide for hours with just one flap of its wings. When it spots its prey, it dives down to catch it at an amazing speed of almost 200 miles per hour!

As well as good eyesight, the golden eagle also has sharp claws for catching and killing its prey.

The toughest part of the swallow's journey is crossing the Mediterreanean Sea.

The **shag** is a bird from the cormorant family. It's very good at fishing. It can often be seen standing on a rock, drying out its feathers.

The **northern gannet** dives into the sea to catch its food. It can reach a top speed of almost 60 miles per hour.

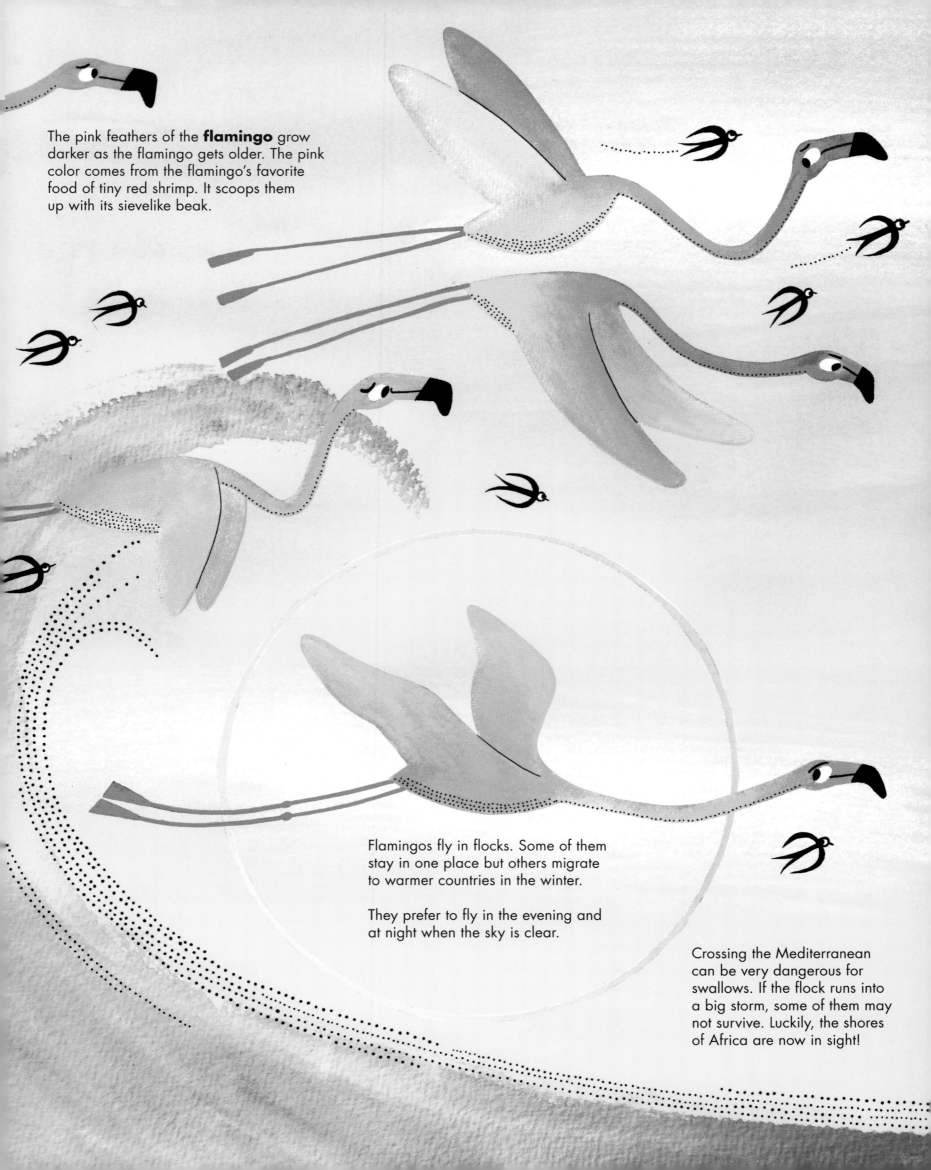

The pink feathers of the **flamingo** grow darker as the flamingo gets older. The pink color comes from the flamingo's favorite food of tiny red shrimp. It scoops them up with its sievelike beak.

Flamingos fly in flocks. Some of them stay in one place but others migrate to warmer countries in the winter.

They prefer to fly in the evening and at night when the sky is clear.

Crossing the Mediterranean can be very dangerous for swallows. If the flock runs into a big storm, some of them may not survive. Luckily, the shores of Africa are now in sight!

The swallows have reached the Sahara Desert. It's a difficult stage in their journey, because there's nowhere to rest, it's hard to find water and it's always very hot.

The distance from one tip of a bird's wings to the other is called its **wingspan**.

The white stork has a wingspan of up to 7 feet. However, its body is very light because its bones are hollow. In fact, most birds have hollow bones, which means that they are light enough to fly.

The **white stork** migrates from Europe to Africa at the end of the summer. It uses warm air currents to lift it up as it flies.

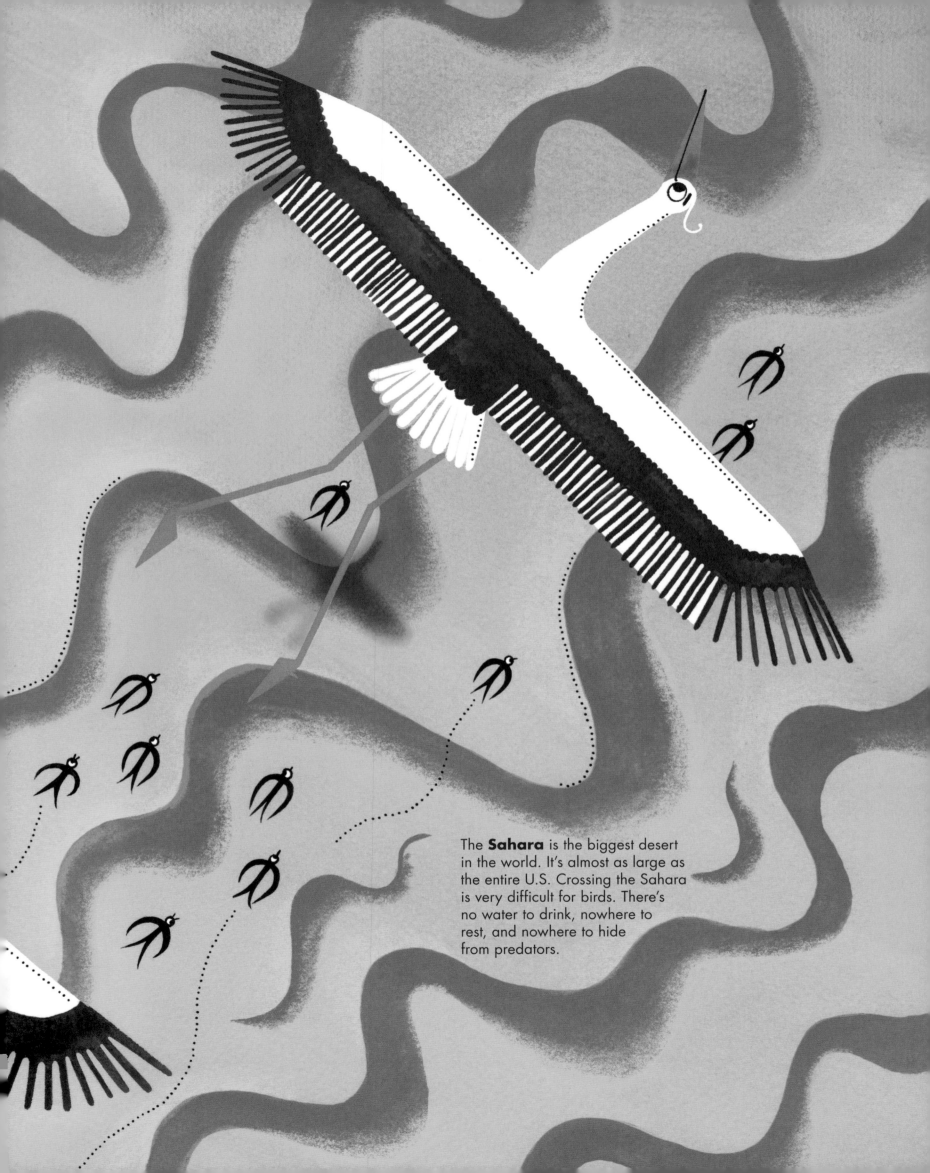

The **Sahara** is the biggest desert in the world. It's almost as large as the entire U.S. Crossing the Sahara is very difficult for birds. There's no water to drink, nowhere to rest, and nowhere to hide from predators.

Finally the swallows have arrived in Africa! Now they are south of the **Equator**, an imaginary line that runs around the middle of the Earth. When it's winter north of the Equator, it's summer in the south.

The **ostrich** is the largest bird in the world. It can grow up to 9 feet tall. It's too heavy to fly but its legs are long and strong so it can run very fast. It flaps its wings to keep itself cool, and also to attract a mate.

Despite what you may have heard, the ostrich never buries its head in the sand. But it often keeps its head close to the ground, looking out for tasty sprouts to eat.

The **secretary bird** has long legs and a crest of feathers on the back of its head. It runs very fast before it takes off, kind of like a plane on a runway. It spends most of its time on the ground, looking for insects and small animals to eat.

The **marabout stork** has no feathers on its head or neck. This is because it often feeds on **carrion**, the bodies of dead animals. Its bald head is easier to keep clean when it's picking meat from their bones.

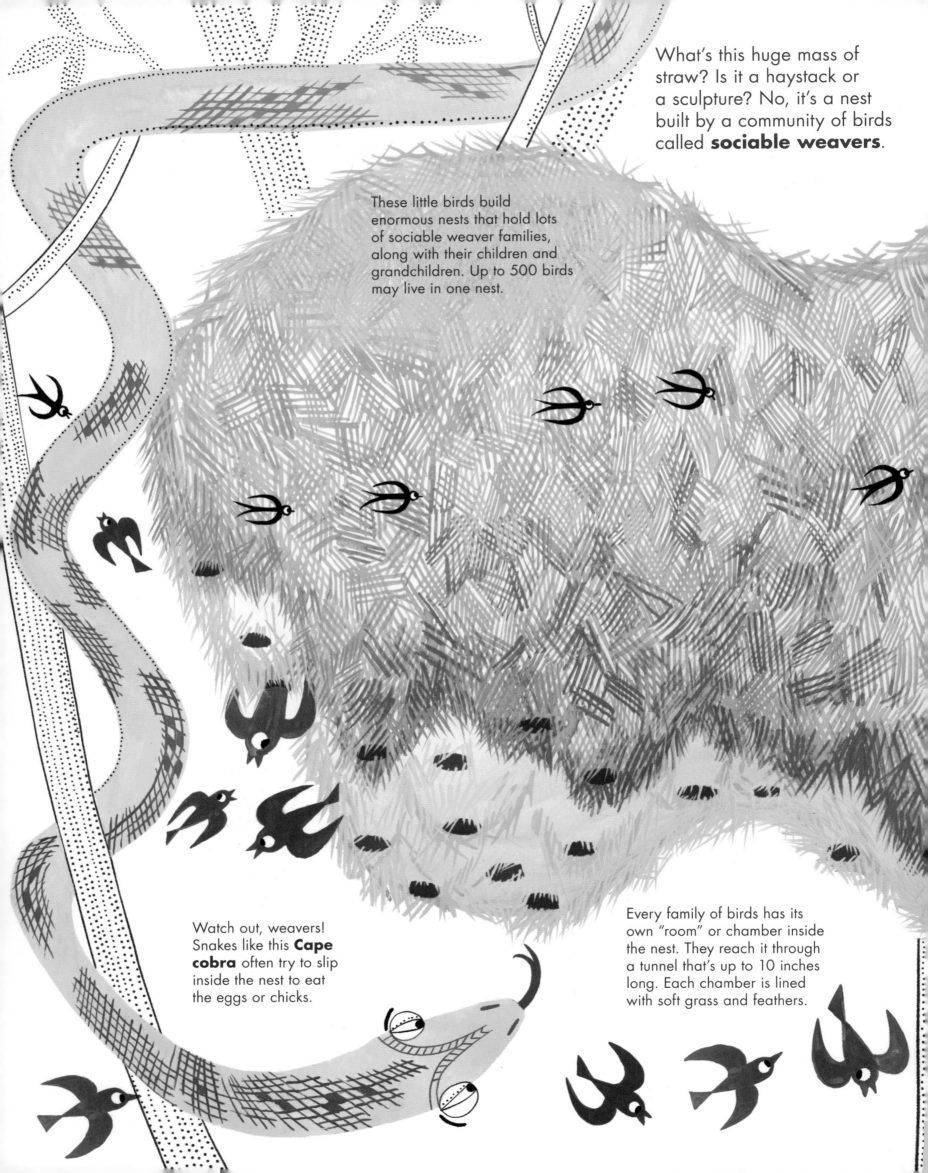

What's this huge mass of straw? Is it a haystack or a sculpture? No, it's a nest built by a community of birds called **sociable weavers**.

These little birds build enormous nests that hold lots of sociable weaver families, along with their children and grandchildren. Up to 500 birds may live in one nest.

Watch out, weavers! Snakes like this **Cape cobra** often try to slip inside the nest to eat the eggs or chicks.

Every family of birds has its own "room" or chamber inside the nest. They reach it through a tunnel that's up to 10 inches long. Each chamber is lined with soft grass and feathers.

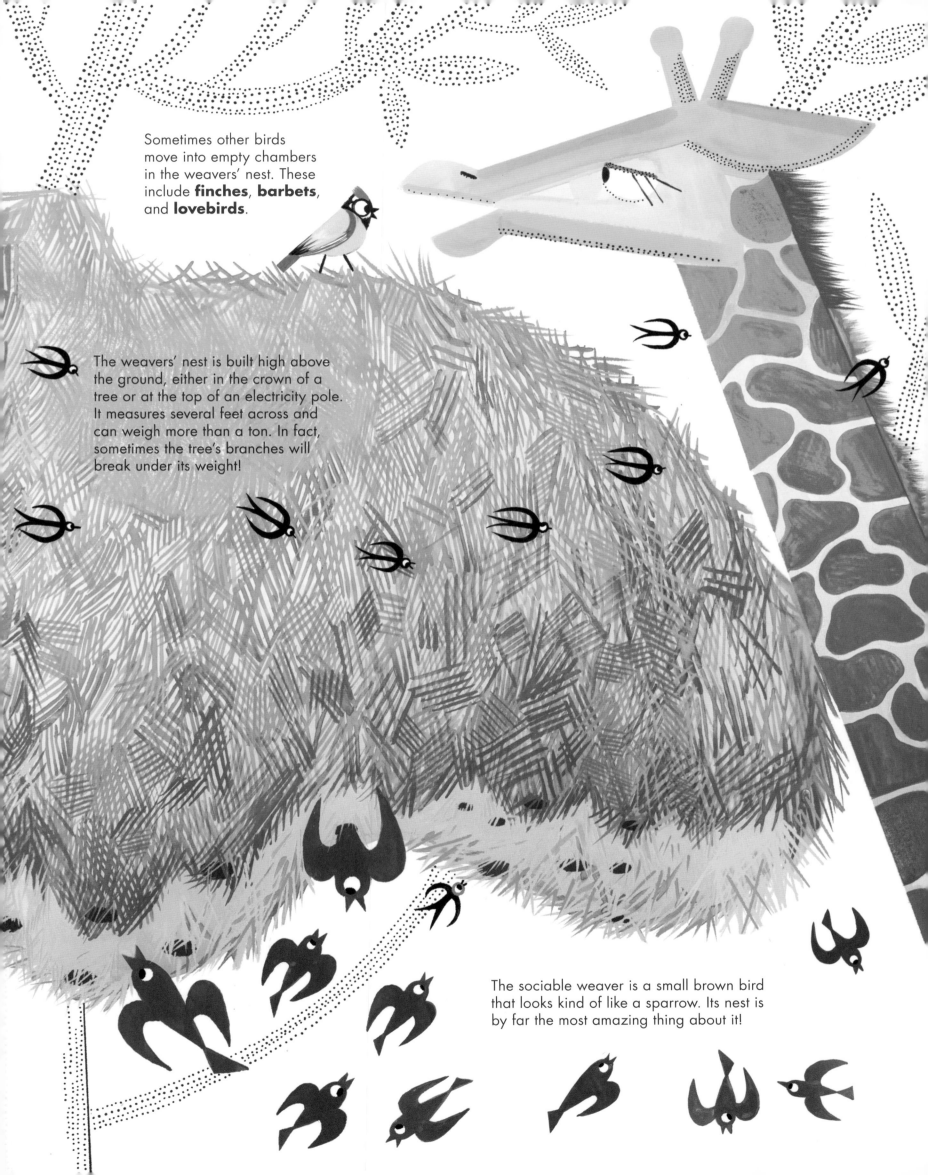

Sometimes other birds move into empty chambers in the weavers' nest. These include **finches**, **barbets**, and **lovebirds**.

The weavers' nest is built high above the ground, either in the crown of a tree or at the top of an electricity pole. It measures several feet across and can weigh more than a ton. In fact, sometimes the tree's branches will break under its weight!

The sociable weaver is a small brown bird that looks kind of like a sparrow. Its nest is by far the most amazing thing about it!

It's easy for swallows to find food on the plains of Africa. They eat lots and lots before they fly north again in the spring.

Swallows migrate back to Europe in the spring, in time for their nesting season. This starts in April and lasts for around five months.

While they're in Africa, swallows like to perch in reed beds. Lots of insects live there, which make an excellent meal. This is important because the swallows need to eat a lot to build up fuel for their flight north.

This beautiful bird is a **gray crowned crane**. It makes its nest near marshes, rivers, and lakes. Because the places where it likes to live are under threat, it is classified as an endangered species.

Wherever we go, it feels like we're surrounded by birds! However, many of them are in danger from traffic and pollution, from the destruction of places where they live, and from the use of chemicals that kill the insects they eat. We humans need to think about what we can do to help and protect all the birds that share our planet.

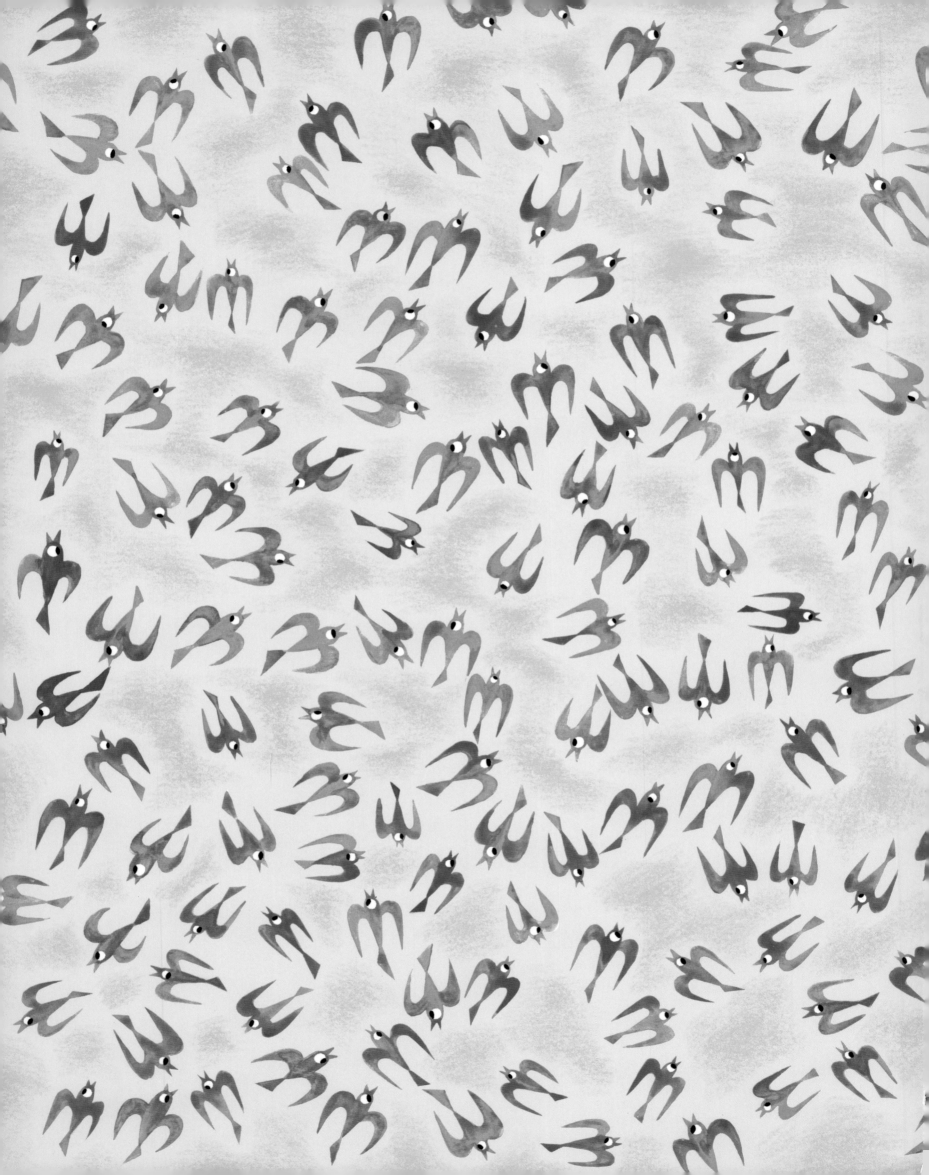